A NOTE TO PARENTS

When your children are ready to "step into reading," giving them the right books—and lots of them—is as crucial as giving them the right food to eat. **Step into Reading Books** present exciting stories and information reinforced with lively, colorful illustrations that make learning to read fun, satisfying, and worthwhile. They are priced so that acquiring an entire library of them is affordable. And they are beginning readers with an important difference—they're written on four levels.

Step 1 Books, with their very large type and extremely simple vocabulary, have been created for the very youngest readers. **Step 2 Books** are both longer and slightly more difficult. **Step 3 Books,** written to mid-second-grade reading levels, are for the child who has acquired even greater reading skills. **Step 4 Books** offer exciting nonfiction for the increasingly proficient reader.

Children develop at different ages. **Step into Reading Books,** with their four levels of reading, are designed to help children become good—and interested—readers *faster.* The grade levels assigned to the four steps—preschool through grade 1 for Step 1, grades 1 through 3 for Step 2, grades 2 and 3 for Step 3, and grades 2 through 4 for Step 4—are intended only as guides. Some children move through all four steps very rapidly; others climb the steps over a period of several years. These books will help your child "step into reading" in style!

To Judy—S.B.

To Eleanor Anderson, who works so well with kids—M.D.

With thanks to Paul L. Sieswerda of the New York Aquarium and Dr. Daniel Odell of Sea World

Library of Congress Cataloging-in-Publication Data
Bokoske, Sharon.
Dolphins! / by Sharon Bokoske and Margaret Davidson ; illustrated by Courtney.
    p.   cm.—(Step into reading. A Step 2 book)
SUMMARY: Introduces dolphins and their physical characteristics, behavior, social structure, intelligence, and interaction with humans.   ISBN 0-679-84437-6 (pbk.)—ISBN 0-679-94437-0 (lib. bdg.)
1. Dolphins—Juvenile literature. [1. Dolphins.] I. Davidson, Margaret, 1936– . II. Courtney, ill.
III. Title.   IV. Series: Step into reading. Step 2 book.
QL737.C432B66   1993   599.5'3—dc20   92-35845

Manufactured in the United States of America   10 9 8 7 6 5 4 3

STEP INTO READING is a trademark of Random House, Inc.

Step into Reading

By Sharon Bokoske
and Margaret Davidson

Illustrated by Courtney

A Step 2 Book

Random House 🏠 New York

One night a woman fell

from a boat into the ocean.

No one saw her fall.

The waves were rough.

Soon she grew tired.

Then something bumped against her.

"A shark!" she thought. "Oh, no!"

It wasn't a shark.

It was a dolphin.

Gently, it pushed her

toward shallow water.

At last she crawled up

on a sandy beach.

The dolphin had saved her life!

There are many amazing stories
about dolphins and people.
People have liked dolphins
for thousands of years.
Ancient artists liked to
draw and paint
dolphins.

Dolphins seem to like us too.

Some dolphins come close to shore.

They swim right up to people.

At one beach in Australia

dolphins let people pet them.

What does a dolphin feel like?

A wet rubber ball!

These dolphins help fishermen.

The fishermen throw out their nets.

The dolphins chase the fish
right in!

Dolphins spend their whole lives
in water.

But they are not fish.

Fish can breathe in water.

Dolphins cannot.

blowhole

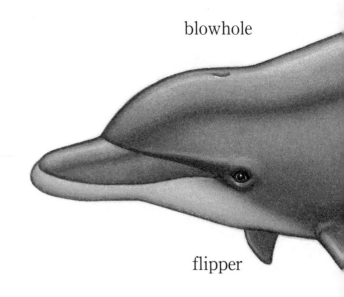

flipper

Dolphins are mammals, like us.

They breathe through a hole

on top of their heads.

fin

flipper

It's called a blowhole.

Dolphins pop up about twice

a minute for a quick breath of air.

Dolphins live all over the world.
There are more than
thirty different kinds.

BOUTO

COMMON DOLPHIN

RISSO'S DOLPHIN

HOURGLASS

BOTTLENOSE

The bottlenose dolphin

is the one people know best.

It has a big built-in grin!

What do dolphins eat?

Fish.

And they are good

at catching them.

A dolphin can find a tiny fish

even if it's too dark to see.

It uses echolocation (ek-o-lo-KAY-shun).

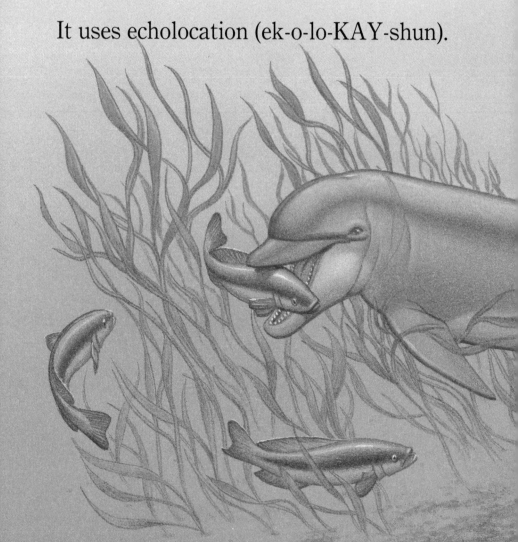

How does echolocation work?

A dolphin sends out

bursts of sound.

CREEEAK.

The sound hits a rock or a fish

or anything else in the water.

Then an echo comes back

to the dolphin.

It's like a picture—

but made with sounds.

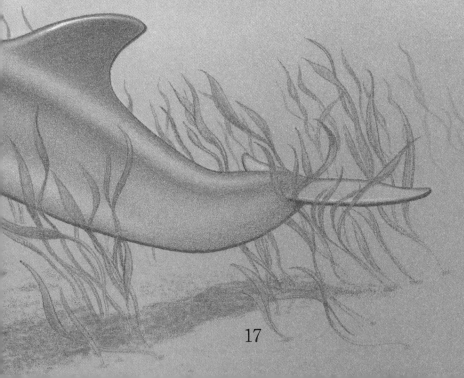

Dolphins are playful.

They will turn almost anything

into a toy.

They toss seaweed and fish.

They like to surf too.

They even hitch rides

on waves made by motorboats!

Dolphins are usually gentle.

But sometimes they get angry.

How can you tell?

The dolphin makes

a loud clapping noise

with its jaws.

Or slaps the water hard with its tail.

Dolphins live in groups.

They help each other out.

Sometimes a dolphin gets sick.

Or hurt.

It sinks in the water—

and can't come up for air.

It could drown!

Other dolphins gather around.

They swim under

the sick dolphin.

They push it up and down
until it can swim by itself.

Sharks and killer whales eat
dolphins—especially babies.

If a shark comes by,
the dolphins circle around it
to scare it away.
If that doesn't work,
the dolphins will fight.

Dolphins can't always
help each other.
Many dolphins swim
with schools of tuna.
When fishermen closed
their tuna nets,
they trapped dolphins too.
Millions of dolphins died.

Many people were upset.

They stopped eating tuna.

Children sent letters to tuna companies.

They begged them to help the dolphins.

At last many companies listened.

Now their fishermen must not trap dolphins.

They mark their cans Dolphin Safe.

But the fight is not over.

People are still working to keep

dolphins safe in the sea.

Around fifty years ago, people
wanted to learn more about dolphins.
So they built big saltwater pools.
They put dolphins inside.
Now scientists could study them
up close.

What did they find out?

Every dolphin is different.

Some are shy.

Some show off.

Some like to tease.

One dolphin liked to yank
the tail feathers of a pelican.
The pelican didn't think
it was funny.
But the dolphin did!

Another dolphin liked to play

with a big sea turtle.

All the turtle wanted to do was sleep.

But the dolphin had other plans.

She spent hours swimming

around her pool—

with the turtle on her back!

Dolphins learn fast.
They have been trained to

raise flags,

shake hands,

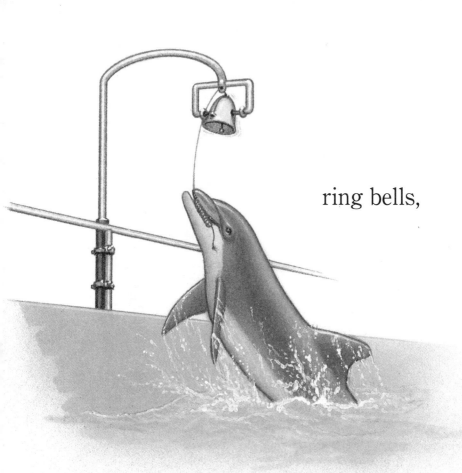

ring bells,

and bat balls.

These two dolphins zip
under water with their trainer.
They rocket him high
into the air!

One dolphin even learned

to paint pictures.

He picks his own brush.

He picks the colors too.

Dolphins have good memories.

A dolphin named Kathy had

a favorite toy.

It was a small rubber ring.

One day a visitor came to watch her.

Kathy flipped her ring to him.

He threw it back.

They played catch

for almost an hour.

Two years later,

the same man came back.

The minute Kathy saw him

she tossed her ring right to him!

Dolphins make

lots of sounds.

Squeak and squawk.

Click and clack.

Rasp and squeal and bleat.

What do these sounds mean?

Many people think dolphins

are talking to each other.

But we don't know for sure.

We know one thing.

Every dolphin has

a one-of-a-kind whistle.

It is like the dolphin's name.

If a baby strays, its mother gives

her special whistle.

The baby whistles back.

Soon they are swimming

side by side again.

Can dolphins understand
human words?
Not really.
But scientists have taught dolphins
hand signs that stand for words.
Dolphins learned words like *Frisbee*,
basket, *right*, *left*, *over*, and *under*.
They learned more than forty words!

This dolphin is watching her trainer.

The trainer makes the hand signs

for *basket*, *right*, *Frisbee*, and *fetch*.

The dolphin knows what that means.

She swims to the Frisbee on her right.

Then she takes it to the basket!

Dolphins can even
answer questions.
There are two paddles
in the dolphin pool.
The white paddle means "yes."
The black paddle means "no."
The trainer asks the dolphin
if there's a ball in this pool.

The dolphin looks all around.

Then she points

to the white paddle.

"Yes," she is saying.

She is right!

There is a keyboard in this pool.

The keyboard has nine buttons on it.

The dolphins use it to ask for things.

They can ask for a fish, a rub,

a ring, or a ball.

What do they ask for the most?

That depends on the dolphin!

What else can dolphins learn?
The Navy once trained
a dolphin named Tuffy.
He made deliveries to scientists
in a deep underwater lab.
He was their mailman!

Dolphins can learn to find

things that are lost underwater.

These dolphins swim with children
who have special problems.
Some of the children are blind.
Some can't walk.
Some can't hear.

The dolphins seem to understand.

They play with the children.

They take them for rides.

And they are always gentle.

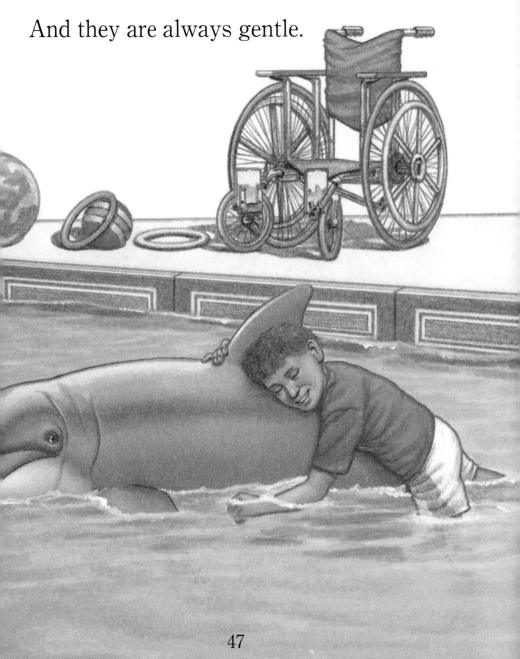

Dolphins and people

live in different worlds.

We don't speak the same language.

But we do share one thing.

A very special friendship!